THE REFORM PARTY

ROSS PEROT
and PAT BUCHANAN

Tricia Andryszewski

THE MILLBROOK PRESS
Brookfield, Connecticut

Published by The Millbrook Press, Inc.
2 Old New Milford Road
Brookfield, CT   06804
www.millbrookpress.com

Library of Congress Cataloging-in-Publication Data
Andryszewski, Tricia. 1956-
The Reform Party : Ross Perot, and Pat Buchanan / Tricia Andryszewski.
p. cm. — (Headliners)
Includes bibliographical references and index.
Summary: Recounts the history of the Reform Party with brief biographies
of its two most visible presidential candidates.
ISBN 0-7613-1906-9 (Library binding : alk. paper)
1. Reform Party (U.S.)—History—Juvenile literature. 2. Presidential candi-
dates—United States—Biography—Juvenile literature. [1. Reform Party
(U.S.) 2. Presidential candidates.] I. Title. II. Series.
JK2391.R64 A53 1999
324.273'8—dc21 99-087456

Cover photographs courtesy of © Robert Maass/Corbis

Photographs courtesy of Corbis/Sygma: p. 4; AP/Wide World Photos: pp.
6, 22, 24, 28, 40, 43, 53; Sygma: pp. 9 (© J. P. Laffont), 15, 37 (© David
Woo/*The Dallas Morning News*); David Woo/*The Dallas Morning News*: p.
11; Liaison Agency: p. 12 (© Terry Ashe); Reuters/Archive Photos: pp. 16
(© John Kuntz), 34 (© Lou Dematteis), 49 (© Eric Miller); Corbis: pp. 18
(© Robert Maass); Corbis/Reuters: p. 32; © AFP/Corbis: p. 46

Contents

Introduction

The Reform Party's New Candidate

Pat Buchanan announcing his departure from the Republican Party and his intention to run for president on the Reform Party ticket.

"Good morning. Today I am ending my lifelong membership in the Republican Party, ... and I am declaring my intention to seek the nomination of the Reform Party for the presidency of the United States....

"Our two [Republican and Democratic] parties have become nothing but two wings on the same bird of prey.... Only the Reform Party offers the hope of a real debate and a real choice of destinies for our country."

With these words, in October 1999, the feisty conservative commentator Pat Buchanan announced that he intended to merge his own political organization with the Reform Party. The Buchanan Brigades, as he often called his supporters, had propelled him through two previous runs for the presidency—as a Republican, in 1992 and 1996. The Reform Party had been the vehicle for billionaire Ross Perot's presidential ambitions during those same elections.

The Reform Party in the 1990s was not so much a movement based on ideas as an organization built around individual candidates. First and foremost, it was the party of Ross Perot, who spent tens of millions of dollars of his own money to build the party through his 1992 and 1996 presidential campaigns and beyond. In 1998, the Reform Party also became the party of Jesse Ventura, the former pro wrestler who was elected governor of Minnesota that year on a Reform Party ticket. Early in the 2000 presidential race, Pat Buchanan decided to make it his party, too.

Both the Reform Party and Pat Buchanan have appealed to voters who feel that the Washington establishment—Republican and Democratic—has lost touch with ordinary Americans and become corrupted by rich and powerful special interests. But unlike the Reform Party, Pat Buchanan has pushed aggressively conservative positions on such social issues as abortion and affirmative action. By joining the Reform Party and seeking its nomination, Buchanan undertook to combine his followers with Reform Party voters into a larger bloc of voters. Together, Pat Buchanan and the Reform Party would take on America's two-party political system in 2000, aiming to create a strong third alternative to the long-established Democrats and Republicans.

This book explains how the Reform Party started and what it and Pat Buchanan have each stood for, especially in the 1992 and 1996 election campaigns. It also offers some informed guesses about how the Reform Party will likely fare in the 2000 presidential election campaign and beyond.

Ross Perot and the Reform Party set out to change America's political system. Pat Buchanan intends to see that it happens. Will the Reform Party fizzle in 2000, becoming just a footnote in history books, like third-party movements in the past? Or will it succeed in becoming a permanent and powerful part of the American political scene?

Chapter 1

Ross Perot, Founder of the Reform Party

Any look at the Reform Party has to begin with the quirky billionaire Ross Perot. Perot's great wealth and his 1992 and 1996 presidential campaigns created the Reform Party. Heading into the 2000 campaign season, Perot remained the party's key behind-the-scenes leader.

Early Life

Henry Ray (later Ross) Perot was born in Texarkana, Texas, on June 27, 1930, the third and youngest child of a small-scale cotton broker. The Perots' first child, a son, died at age three, before Ross and his older sister, Bette, were born.

Perot graduated from the U.S. Naval Academy in 1953 and then went to sea. In 1955, he sought an early

Opposite: Perot poses for a photographer in a computer room at EDS in 1968.

release from the Navy, complaining about sailors' "god-lessness," drunkenness, and sexual promiscuity. "I find it unsatisfying to live, work and be directed in an atmosphere where taking God's name in vain is a part of the everyday vocabulary," he wrote in a letter to his congressman. In the end, though, Perot served his entire four-year tour of duty.

Perot next sold computers, very successfully, for IBM in Dallas for several years. He founded his own computer services company, Electronic Data Systems (EDS), in 1962. In the late 1960s, EDS expanded and became a very profitable big business, largely on the strength of its contracts with state governments to process paperwork connected with the then-new Medicare and Medicaid government-paid health care programs. EDS also became known as a very conservative place to work: Perot insisted that his employees wear unfashionably conservative business clothes and hairstyles and accept company policy banning homosexuality and adultery.

Billionaire Perot

Ross Perot (as he prefers to be called) became a very wealthy man—a billionaire by 1968. He continued to expand his business interests and became something of a public figure and philanthropist, taking interest in causes as diverse as the problems of Vietnam veterans and improving Texas public schools. Since the late 1960s, Perot has persistently supported the cause of those who believe that U.S. prisoners of war are still being held in Southeast Asia, decades after the Vietnam War ended. In 1979, Perot hired a team of commandos to free two EDS employees who were in jail in Iran. Their lucky and successful mission became the subject of a made-for-television movie.

Perot visiting a camp for American prisoners of war in Vietnam, 1969.

In 1984, Perot sold EDS to General Motors (GM), but he remained the company's administrative head. The marriage between Perot and GM was not a happy one, and GM bought him out in 1986. Perot then founded two new companies, Perot Systems Corporation and Perot Group.

Perot has been married, since 1956, to Margot Birmingham Perot. They have five children.

In February and March 1992, Perot suddenly became a center of national attention when he suggested, on

—from Ross Perot's memoirs,
My Life and the Principles for Success

"I grew up during the Depression. We lived in a house that cost four thousand dollars. Our house did not have a washing machine, so my mother washed all of our clothes by hand, scrubbing them on a washboard…. My dad worked, saved his money, and bought the house only when he could pay cash for it. Throughout my childhood, he taught me never to buy anything on credit. His words were, 'Figure out what you want. Save your money, and when you can afford it, buy it.' He emphasized that looking forward to buying something was as much fun, if not more fun, than actually owning it….

"When I was six years old, I really wanted a bicycle. My dad looked at me, smiled, and said, 'Son, work, save your money and buy a bicycle.' It may seem unthinkable that a six-year-old should work, but during the Depression it was normal. This started my business training….

"The first decision I made was that I would buy a secondhand bicycle because it cost less. I sold flower seeds and Christmas cards and made enough money to buy my first bicycle for five dollars. I cannot convey the excitement and anticipation I had during the weeks and months that I was selling things to earn enough money to buy that bicycle. I will never forget the day I bought it, but just as my dad had predicted, three or four days later, it was simply something that I now owned. In fact, it had been a lot more fun to look forward to it than it was to own it. I rode this bicycle all through high school and used it on paper routes and other jobs."

Ross Perot and his family in April 1986.

cable television's *Larry King Live*, that he would run for president if his supporters arranged for his name to go on the ballot in all fifty states. At a time when much of the public was fed up with more conventional politicians, Perot mania took off like a rocket.

Who Is Pat Buchanan?

Born on November 2, 1938, in Washington, D.C., Patrick Joseph Buchanan was the third of his family's nine children. His father was an accountant, and both of his parents were devout Catholics. Pat Buchanan attended Catholic elementary and high schools in Washington and suburban Maryland, and won a scholarship to Georgetown University, where he majored in English and philosophy. After college, Buchanan earned a master's degree at Columbia University's School of Journalism in New York City. In 1962, he went to work for a newspaper in St. Louis.

Conservative Pundit and Politician

By the mid-1960s, Buchanan was seriously interested in conservative politics. He wanted to see a conservative Republican elected president, and he believed that

Opposite:
Richard Nixon and his new speechwriter, Pat Buchanan.

— from Pat Buchanan's memoirs, *Right From the Beginning*

"We, my three closest brothers and I, were 'raised Catholic' in the '40s and '50s. . . . On Sundays, my father and mother guaranteed we never missed Mass. We were all awakened at eight o'clock, and all four of the older boys were outfitted in matching brown slacks, brown caps, and camel's-hair coats, and so presented at nine-o'clock Mass. Mom would stay home, fix breakfast for us when we got back at ten, and then hurry to make the eleven o'clock herself. . . .

"While believing in that Catholic faith was no guarantee of superior behavior . . . it did provide us with what our non-Catholic friends did not have: a code of morality, a code of conduct, a sure knowledge of right and wrong, a way of acknowledging personal guilt and of seeking out and attaining forgiveness and absolution. We had a hierarchy of values; we knew where we were going and how to get there; even in childhood, we were not confused. We had certitude....

"[At] the Buchanan Dinner Table Debating Forum . . . every one of us was opinionated; and we were all taught not to back down. . . . If you never quit an argument, presumably you never lost. To make oneself heard as the argument got intense, we got louder and louder....

"On one occasion, which lives in family lore as 'The Easter Massacre,' [the dinner-table argument] degenerated into a fistfight between [two of the brothers].... My father and I finally separated the fighters. Then, I noticed Mom heading into the kitchen near tears at how her sumptuous Easter dinner, which had taken days to prepare, had ended in ruin and rancor. Pop followed her, and I could hear him saying, 'Catherine, don't worry about it; these things always happen when you raise strong boys.' He felt it a natural manifestation of healthy competitive family spirit."

Pat Buchanan, on the left in the back row, poses with his brothers and sisters for this undated family portrait.

In August 1992, Pat Buchanan and his sister and campaign manager Bay prepare for the Republican National Convention, at which Buchanan will speak.

Richard Nixon (who had lost the 1960 presidential race to Democrat John Kennedy) had the best chance of winning in 1968. Buchanan persuaded Nixon to hire him at the beginning of 1966. He wrote speeches and organized press coverage during the campaign and continued to advise and write speeches after Nixon won the election and moved into the White House. Buchanan, who was apparently in no way involved in the Watergate scandal that ended Nixon's presidency, remained at the White House to work for Nixon's successor, President Gerald Ford.

In 1975, Buchanan left the White House to express his conservative political and social views in a syndicated newspaper column. The column was a success, and in 1978 he branched out into talk radio and eventually television. He became best known for his confrontational, combative style and for his sharp attacks on both liberal Democrats and Republicans who were not as ultraconservative as he is.

In 1985, Buchanan returned to the White House and became President Ronald Reagan's communications director. He briefly considered running for the 1988 Republican presidential nomination but decided against it. Instead, he returned to private life in 1987, picking up his talk-show and newspaper-column career again. In 1991, he began running for the 1992 Republican nomination for president.

Pat Buchanan has been married to Shelley Ann Scarney, a former Nixon staffer, since 1971. The couple have no children and live in upscale, suburban McLean, Virginia, just outside Washington, D.C. Buchanan has an especially close relationship with his sister Angela "Bay" Buchanan, who has been his chief political adviser.

Chapter 3

The 1992 Presidential Campaign

In December 1991, Pat Buchanan announced that he would challenge incumbent President George Bush for the Republican nomination in the 1992 election campaign. Buchanan promised to "put America first" and attacked Bush ("King George," he called him) for being out of touch with ordinary working Americans, for compromising too much with Democrats in Congress, and—especially—for raising taxes in a "seedy backroom deal with the big spenders on Capitol Hill." Campaigning in late 1991 and early 1992, Buchanan favored

- freezing federal spending at current levels,
- cutting taxes for the middle class,
- halting for two years any new federal regulations affecting businesses,

Opposite:
Pat Buchanan, campaigning in Texas, does as the Texans do and wears that 10-gallon hat.

- banning abortion,
- slashing foreign aid,
- punishing countries with trade policies that hurt the United States, and
- restricting immigration to protect the country's "Euro-American" character.

Buchanan presented himself as a populist—a politician working for the good of common people rather than the rich and powerful. (Most Republicans work to strengthen business and assert that a strong economy is best for everyone.) But woven into Buchanan's populist appeal was an angry, negative, ominous element. Intentionally or not, Buchanan encouraged bigotry against outsiders— hatred of blacks and Hispanics, feminists and homosexuals, foreigners, Asians, and Jews. Critics claimed Buchanan himself was a bigot—a charge he hotly denied.

In February 1992, Buchanan won 37 percent of the vote in the New Hampshire Republican primary—a surprisingly strong showing against an incumbent president. (President Bush took 53 percent of the vote, other candidates 10 percent.) Polls of people who had just voted indicated that a majority of those who voted for Buchanan did so to "send a message" to Washington: The economy was ailing, unemployment had tripled in New Hampshire since 1988, people were worried about big business shipping their jobs overseas, and neither Congress nor the president were dealing with these problems effectively.

Buchanan continued to rack up about one-third of the vote in primary after primary in early March. (He did less well, however, in states where he split the anti-immigration, anti-minority extremist vote with former Ku Klux Klan leader David Duke.) But he failed to actually win even one state. By "Super Tuesday," March 10, when Republican primaries were held in eight states, it was clear that George Bush would be the Republican nominee.

Buchanan soon acknowledged this and said he would stop attacking Bush in an effort to avoid hurting the Republicans' chances in November. But he vowed to keep his campaign alive through the Republican National Convention in August.

Pat Buchanan's strong appeal to lower-income and religious Republican conservatives divided the party and made Bush look weak. Although Buchanan failed to come even close to gaining the nomination, he succeeded in pushing issues he cared about (particularly abortion) to the top of the Republican party's agenda. Moderate Republicans were dismayed—and worried that a weakened George Bush might not be able to beat a moderate Democrat in the fall.

Perot Jumps In

Although Buchanan lost the race early in the primary season, the public discontent he appealed to didn't fade away. Many voters (perhaps most) were uninspired by both of the front-runner candidates, Republican George Bush and Arkansas's Democratic Governor Bill Clinton. Many felt fed up with "gridlock" politics—the endless bickering between Democrats and Republicans in Washington that prevented serious work on solving the nation's problems. Washington seemed corrupt, incompetent, and out of touch with the rest of the country. The time was ripe for an independent candidate—neither Republican nor Democrat—to appeal to America's alienated, fed-up voters.

On March 18, independent billionaire Ross Perot affirmed that he would run for president if his supporters got him on the ballot in all fifty states—an effort that was by then well under way. Presenting himself as an outsider,

"Watch my lips," was a response that got a good chuckle from reporters when they asked whether Perot would be running for president in '92.

he criticized the Washington establishment, speaking in a colorful, folksy way that delighted the public: "In plain Texas talk," he said, "it's time to take out the trash and clean out the barn." He promised that, if he were president, he'd get rid of the federal budget deficit "without breaking a sweat," and he'd fix America's ailing economy and political system: "We'll be going night and day. We'll have that car jacked up, we'll have the engine out of it, we'll be working on it, and get it back on the road." Perot boosted his credibility considerably by promising to spend as much as $50 to $100 million of his own money on his campaign.

By the end of the month, 16 percent of voters polled said they'd vote for Perot if the election were held that day. (President Bush was favored by 44 percent, Democrat Bill Clinton by 31 percent.) As early as late April, some polls showed Perot actually winning the election. Through late spring into summer, many polls showed all three candidates with about one-third of the vote each—a race too close to call.

As Perot's popularity rose, so did criticism of him. The chief complaint was that he was too vague about where he stood on various issues. Concerns were also raised about his character and temperament. Critics said he was too thin-skinned, gullible, unreliable, and, well, too flaky to be president:

- A Texas newspaper claimed that, in response to negative coverage about a business deal involving Perot's son, Perot had threatened to disclose details concerning the sex life of one of the paper's reporters.

- Perot claimed that assassins hired by North Vietnam had targeted himself and his family between 1969 and 1973.

- Newspapers reported that Perot, in 1981, had proposed setting up an airplane refueling service for drug smugglers in the Caribbean that would feed information to the U.S. Customs Service.

- Numerous reports emerged that Perot had hired private investigators to look into the lives of various politicians, employees, and even his own children.

In early May, Perot announced that he was reducing his public appearances so he could organize his campaign and develop "carefully thought-out positions on each of the major issues." In June and July, Perot began to state positions on certain issues, but critics still complained that what he was offering was incomplete.

Perot Drops Out

Through spring and into summer, as the public came to know Perot better, the number of people who viewed him negatively rose—more than doubling, according to one poll, from 9 percent in April to 20 percent in late June. In early July, the number who said they'd vote for Perot was dropping like a stone—to just 20 percent on July 15, according to one poll, down 10 percentage points in just one week.

On July 16, the last day of the Democratic National Convention that nominated Arkansas Governor Bill

A dismayed campaign worker learns that Perot has pulled out of the presidential race.

Clinton for president, Ross Perot announced that he was ending his presidential campaign, which had never been officially declared. He said that the unexpectedly "revitalized" Democratic party would make it impossible for him to win in November.

Perot's supporters were stunned and outraged when he quit. With months of hard work (and more than $6.4 million of Perot's money) they had painstakingly collected millions of signatures to get him on the ballot. Perot urged his supporters to continue that effort so their concerns about reforming government would stay on the national agenda.

Buchanan at the Republican Convention

While Perot was still flying high, through late spring into summer, Pat Buchanan continued to win as much as a quarter of the vote in Republican primary elections against President Bush. Buchanan insisted that he had earned the right to speak at the Republican National Convention—and warned that scores of delegates loyal to him would disrupt the convention unless he was heard. Republican leaders loyal to President Bush weren't happy about giving Buchanan such a prominent moment in the national spotlight. But in the end they agreed that if Buchanan endorsed and asked his supporters to vote for Bush, he would be allowed to speak.

On the evening of August 17, Pat Buchanan addressed the Republican National Convention and, through television, a prime-time audience of millions of Americans. In addition to endorsing President Bush's bid for reelection, Buchanan took swipes at homosexuals, "radical feminism," and assorted liberal Democrats. Buchanan's supporters and many conservative Christian-Coalition Republicans (then at the height of their power

— from Pat Buchanan's speech to the 1992 Republican National Convention

"Tonight I want to talk to the 3 million Americans who voted for me [in the Republican primaries]. I will never forget you, nor the great honor you have done me. But I do believe, deep in my heart, that the right place for us to be now—in this presidential campaign—is right beside George Bush. The party is our home; this party is where we belong. And don't let anyone tell you any different....

"This election is about much more than who gets what. It is about who we are. It is about what we believe. It is about what we stand for as Americans. There is a religious war going on in our country for the soul of America. It is a cultural war....

"My friends, in those six months [during my campaign], ... the saddest days were the days of the bloody riot in L.A., the worst in our history....

"Hours after the violence ended I visited the Army compound in south L.A.... [The soldiers there] had come into L.A. late on the second day, and they walked up a dark street, where the mob had looted and burned every building but one, a [nursing] home for the aged. The mob was heading in, to ransack and loot the apartments of the terrified old men and women. When the troopers arrived, M-16s at the ready, the mob threatened and cursed, but the mob retreated. It had met the one thing that could stop it: force, rooted in justice, backed by courage....

"And as they took back the streets of L.A., block by block, so we must take back our cities, and take back our culture, and take back our country.

"God bless you, and God bless America."

in the Republican party) cheered and applauded enthusiastically. However, many who heard the speech were appalled at Buchanan's harshly intolerant tone, and especially at his use of the phrase "cultural war," which translates to "*Kulturkampf*," a buzzword favored by Adolf Hitler.

Buchanan chose to illustrate this "war" with a story about U.S. troops confronting a black "mob" at a nursing home during the rioting and looting that occurred in Los Angeles in April after an all-white jury there failed to convict police officers for beating a black man, Rodney King. (Eyewitnesses have said that the troopers did not in fact confront a "mob" at the nursing home, since they arrived there after looters had left the neighborhood.) The way Buchanan told the story, it sounded very much like the lurid novels about race war (such as *The Turner Diaries*) popular among neo-Nazi white supremacists. Buchanan's critics cited this as evidence that Buchanan was seeking the support of racists by signaling that he secretly agreed with them.

Perot's Return

Within days after dropping his presidential bid in July, Ross Perot began to hint that he might pick it up again. Perot continued to pour millions of dollars into efforts to put his name on the ballot across the country. A campaign manifesto/economic plan that Perot and his advisers had worked on for the past several months, *United We Stand: How We Can Take Back Our Country*, was published in August and was a best-seller by Labor Day.

Perot's plan focused mainly on economic matters. Its centerpiece was a proposal not only to stop the federal government's deficit spending but actually to pay back the national debt (then at $4 trillion and climbing) by cutting spending and raising taxes, mostly on the wealthy. Perot also emphasized political reform ("take back our country") and stated his positions on various other issues, from abortion to education, crime, and race relations.

Balancing the Budget

Congressional
Budget Office
Projection

Perot
Plan

$754 Billion Deficit
Reduction Package

1994   1995   1996   1997   1998

Perot during one of his thirty-minute televised campaign ads. The dozens of simple charts and graphs he used to illustrate his points were hallmarks of his infomercials.

On October 1, with his name on every state ballot, Perot announced that he was back in the race. He said he had to run because neither the Democrats nor the Republicans were addressing the problems described in his book.

This time out, though, Perot's popularity and credibility were much lower. Few people thought he had any chance of winning in November, and the number of those polled who said they'd vote for him hovered at around 10 percent.

Perot embarked on a series of no-nonsense televised infomercials, just him at a desk with charts and graphs and his trademark colorful phrasing. He participated in all three presidential candidates' debates. In the first debate, his plain talk played well: "We've got to clean this mess up, leave this country in good shape, and pass on the American dream" to our children, he said. But in the second and third debates, he seemed cranky and unsure of himself.

Perot continued to run fresh TV infomercials, spending tens of millions of dollars on the effort to get his message out. He began to edge up in the polls a bit—even as he undercut his own gains by making the bizarre statement that a Republican dirty-tricks plan to disrupt his daughter's wedding had influenced his July decision to drop out of the presidential campaign.

Election Day

On Election Day, November 3, 1992, Bill Clinton was elected president of the United States, with 43 percent of the vote. George Bush received 38 percent, Ross Perot 19 percent.

Although Perot lost big, in a sense he won big, too. His 19 percent was more of the vote than any independent or third-party candidate for president had won since 1912, when former president Teddy Roosevelt ran as a Progressive Party candidate and polled 27 percent. (In 1968, independent candidate George Wallace took 13 percent of the vote; in 1980, John Anderson polled 7 percent.) Perot might also have helped Bill Clinton defeat George Bush, by siphoning off voters who would have voted Republican had Perot not been on the ballot. This

— Ross Perot, *United We Stand: How We Can Take Back Our Country*

"The Federal debt is now $4 trillion. That's $4,000,000,000,000. The debt is like a crazy aunt we keep down in the basement. All the neighbors know she's there, but nobody wants to talk about her. . . .

"We are a great nation. We are a people with a great heart. We want to reach out to the single mother struggling to support herself and her children. We want to help the disadvantaged, provide scholarships for deserving students, and make basic health care available to anyone who needs it. Instead, the result of the toil, sacrifice, and dedication of our working people will go into paying the interest on a government debt we shouldn't have created in the first place. . . .

"If anyone wants to know who's to blame for the . . . debt, just go look in the mirror.

"You and I are to blame. You and I are the shareholders of this country. We own it. . . .

"The first words of the Constitution are 'We, the people.' *We* created the Constitution. *We* created Congress. It exists for us, not the other way around. *We* hire and pay for the bureaucracy. *They all work for us.* . . .

"Before we can hope to eliminate our deficit, we have to overhaul the political system that created it. Our Founders built a beautiful ship of state, but the barnacles have latched on and the hull has rusted. It's time for a scrubdown from top to bottom. . . .

"The United States government must pay its way. There are only two ways to do it: reduce spending and generate revenues. It's that simple. . . .

"Government is not a candy store in which every group can pick from any jar it wants. This is not free money. It's your money, and more importantly, it's your children's money. . . .

"We have broken the faith we owe to our children. The politicians can't restore it. Only the people can.

"Only the people, the owners of this country, can make America strong again."

may have suited Perot just fine; it was widely believed that he loathed Bush personally.

As for Buchanan, many Republicans felt that he, too, had helped defeat George Bush. His hard-edged speech-making had widened the division within the Republican party between religious conservatives and more moderate Republicans. After Buchanan's harsh attacks on Bush in the primaries, it must have been hard for his supporters to turn around and vote for Bush in November. How many Buchanan Republicans had simply stayed home on Election Day or voted for Ross Perot?

Chapter 4

NAFTA, a New Party, and the 1996 Presidential Campaign

After the 1992 election, Ross Perot continued his political activities with United We Stand America, the "grass-roots" organization essentially directed by Perot. In March 1993, Perot testified before Congress, demanding government reform and a realistic economic program. Soon, however, he and his organization turned much of their attention to international trade. So did Pat Buchanan.

NAFTA

"You will hear a giant sucking sound." That's what Ross Perot said the North American Free Trade Agreement (NAFTA) would cause—a great rush of American jobs sucked south across the Mexican border. NAFTA was

Perot uses a newspaper ad about NAFTA to make a point during testimony before Congress.

designed to reduce trade barriers between the United States and neighboring Canada and Mexico. Perot claimed that if NAFTA became law, as many as three million U.S. workers would lose their jobs as big corporations sent their work to Mexico, where labor was much cheaper.

Through spring and summer 1993, Perot spoke out and ran television ads blasting NAFTA. In August, Perot and economist Pat Choate published a book on the subject, *Save Your Job, Save Our Country: Why NAFTA Must Be Stopped—Now!*

Buchanan and Perot had support from workers across the country in their opposition to NAFTA, but Congress and President Clinton prevailed.

Pat Buchanan also attacked NAFTA, calling it "a leveraged buyout of American liberty." Working for Republican presidents from Nixon to Reagan, Buchanan had spent much of his career promoting the virtues of free-trade, free-market capitalism—virtues that NAFTA was intended to promote. In his 1992 campaign, though, Buchanan had moved away from the traditional Republican free-trade position into an "America first" kind of economic protectionism. His opposition to NAFTA moved him further still in that direction.

In November 1993, Ross Perot debated NAFTA on television with Vice President Al Gore—and got trounced. NAFTA soon passed Congress and was signed by President Bill Clinton.

Perot in 1994

After NAFTA, Perot turned to criticizing Congress for allowing itself to be distracted by the Whitewater scandal (a failed real estate venture in which Bill and Hillary Clinton had been involved years earlier in Arkansas) instead of tackling issues such as health care reform. Perot also, in early 1994, sharply criticized the Clinton administration's big health care reform plan, saying that it would be a mistake to turn America's health care system over to the government.

In October 1994, Perot asked voters to "send a message" by voting Republican in the November congressional elections. But with that endorsement, he also sent a warning: "I promise you, Mr. and Mrs. America . . . we will create a third party that will deliver" if the Republicans fail to bring about real reform in Washington.

Whether Perot was a factor or not, Republicans that November won control of the U.S. House of Representatives for the first time in forty years. They won a majority in the U.S. Senate, too. Newt Gingrich, an energetic and combative Republican conservative, became the new speaker of the House of Representatives. In the Senate, Robert Dole became the new majority leader. A longtime leader among Republicans in the Senate, Dole was expected to seek his party's nomination for the presidency in 1996.

Buchanan Looks Ahead to 1996

In March 1995, Pat Buchanan announced that he would once again seek the Republican nomination for president. As combative as ever, he spoke of continuing the "revolution" he'd started with his 1992 campaign, the "cultural war" against "custodians of political correctness" and in support of America's Judeo-Christian heritage. Critics once again accused Buchanan of pandering to racists.

Buchanan continued to condemn NAFTA, proposing instead that U.S. jobs and wages be protected by imposing tariffs on foreign-made goods sold in the United States. "We have to ask ourselves as conservatives what it is we want to conserve in America," Buchanan said, speaking of preserving family farms and other family-owned businesses while campaigning toward the end of 1995. "I believe in the market system, but I don't worship at the market system. I don't worship at the altar of efficiency as I believe some so-called conservatives do."

In addition to his protectionist trade policy, Buchanan made uncompromising opposition to abortion a centerpiece of his campaign. He also proposed changes in tax laws, elimination of the U.S. Department of Education, term limits for members of Congress and federal judges, tough measures against illegal immigration (including a "Buchanan fence" at the Mexican border), and a five-year moratorium on *legal* immigration into the United States.

United We Stand Becomes the Reform Party

In August 1995, Ross Perot and United We Stand America hosted a conference in Dallas featuring speeches by assorted presidential hopefuls and other political leaders. Pat Buchanan's speech at that meeting brought the crowd to its feet several times, cheering him on as he attacked NAFTA and other trade agreements, U.S. aid to foreign countries, illegal immigration, and affirmative action.

Pat Buchanan (standing behind Perot) was one of ten presidential hopefuls who spoke at the United We Stand America conference in August '95.

— from letter signed by Ross Perot in an October 1995 newsletter

"Since 1992, the American voters have been very clear about what they want and expect from their elected servants—they want their faith and trust restored in their government.

"Voters remain frustrated because many of their demands have been left unmet by Congress and the White House due to partisan gridlock:

- No plan has been adopted to balance the budget.
- Reforms have not been implemented to change the influence of money in elections.
- Lobbyists continue to buy influence in our government.
- Bankruptcy threatens some of our most important programs such as Medicare and Social Security.

"The failure to meet these demands is not because our elected officials are ineffective—it is because they are working within an ineffective system.

"IT'S TIME TO CHANGE A SYSTEM THAT DOESN'T WORK.

"Today, nearly two-thirds of all American voters are so frustrated with the two-party system that they want a new political party. Half of all Republicans and Democrats are included in this group. . . .

"This political party . . . will belong to the people who build it—not the special interests. . . .

"[It] will make the necessary reforms so the 21st century will be the greatest in our history for our children and grandchildren.

"FINALLY, A POLITICAL PARTY FOR THE INDEPENDENT VOTERS—THE MAJORITY OF AMERICAN VOTERS.

"All it takes is for concerned Americans to come together, get organized and act in the best interest of our country.

"Can one person make the difference?

"YES—*YOU* CAN."

On the last day of the conference, Perot spoke about campaign finance reform, term limits for Congress, and balancing the federal budget. He did not say whether he would run for president in 1996.

Although no consensus emerged at the August convention on forming a third party, the following month

Perot announced that he would do just that. Originally called the Independence Party, its name was soon changed to "Reform" because other groups were already using the "Independence" name in several states. In November, a spokeswoman for the fledgling Reform Party announced that the party would skip the spring 1996 primary elections and instead select its presidential and vice presidential candidates at a convention later in the year.

Go, Pat, Go

By January 1996, only a few candidates for the presidency remained likely possibilities. On the Democratic side, incumbent President Bill Clinton and Vice President Al Gore had their party's nomination sewn up. Ross Perot remained a wild card: He said that he was not interested in running for president, but he hadn't ruled it out. On the Republican side of the campaign, Senator Bob Dole was the front-runner. Among the half-dozen other Republicans still in the race were former Tennessee governor and Bush cabinet member Lamar Alexander, millionaire publishing heir Steve Forbes—and Pat Buchanan.

After squeaking to a narrow victory over Pat Buchanan in the Iowa caucuses, Bob Dole lost the New Hampshire Republican primary to Buchanan on February 20. (Lamar Alexander followed close behind Dole in New Hampshire. The top three candidates were nearly tied.)

Buchanan's win focused fresh attention on the dark side of his candidacy. His campaign drew significant support not only from the large number of disaffected Americans fed up with politics as usual but also from white supremacist and militia-supporting extremists. In several southern states, for example, Buchanan's campaign was aided by the political apparatus developed

Former Klansman David Duke is shown here at a radio station in Miami declaring his intention to run in the '92 presidential election as a Republican. Many of Duke's supporters in 1992 favored Pat Buchanan in 1996.

there by and for the former Klansman/neo-Nazi politician David Duke. Such openly bigoted organizations as Christian Identity Online and the "white racialist" information clearinghouse Stormfront featured the Buchanan campaign on their World Wide Web sites and referred prospective volunteers to the campaign's own Web site.

Buchanan came under increasing pressure to repudiate his ties to the extremist fringe. Eventually, his campaign removed several extremists from leadership positions—most notably Gun Owners of America's Larry Pratt, who had shared the speaker's podium with an assortment of white supremacists at various militia-related rallies and other gatherings. Buchanan reluctantly ousted Pratt as his campaign cochairman in February.

— from Pat Buchanan's speech to the Texas state Republican convention, June 1996

"The nomination battle for the presidency is about more than who gets the nomination. It's also about the heart and soul of a party. . . .

"Three million Republicans, independents, Perot voters, Democrats, voted for Pat Buchanan in the primaries. Many of them did so because they believed in me. . . .

"Four years ago I gave a speech in Houston. . . . I said there was a cultural war going on in this country for the soul of America, and that war is about who we are, what we believe, and what we stand for as people. . . . This cultural struggle, and this struggle for the soul of our country, is going to continue. . . . Our party is approaching a crossroads, I believe, as our society and country are approaching a great crossroads. . . . We need a new party, a new party struggling to be born, and it . . . can be the party of America's future. But . . . we not only gotta know who it is [that] we're against, we know that, but we've got to know what it is that we're for.

"Our country faces some terrible trials ahead, and people ask us, 'How do we decide on this or that issue?' And I tell them, 'Well, we're heading into the future. We've got two great bulwark documents of the past to guide us, one of those is the Constitution of the United States and the other is the Bible, the Old and New Testament.'

"In there, my friends, we have the truths to guide men's lives, the truths that make men free—and the truth that's crushed to earth is gonna rise again. . . . Remember, this is God's country. That's what we want to repair and make great again. God's eyes are on us. . . .

"God bless you all!"

Buchanan's campaign lost momentum not long after the Pratt dismissal. He never received more than 30 percent of the vote in any of the Republican primaries.

From the beginning of March, Bob Dole took decisive command of the race for the Republican nomination. Toward the end of that month, Buchanan conceded that Dole would be the Republican nominee for the presidency. He vowed, however, to keep on campaigning, pushing his political agenda right up to the Republican convention in San Diego that August. (Buchanan, who sometimes called his supporters "peasants with pitchforks," told one Texas crowd in June, "Keep your pitchforks sharp, we're going all the way to San Diego!")

Buchanan was not permitted to speak to the convention, which was carefully scripted to appeal to moderate voters. Nonetheless, he sounded almost gleeful that week. Apparently with an eye on the 2000 race, Buchanan contended that "whole sections" of the ultraconservative Republican party platform drafted that summer—"the [antiabortion] stand for life, protecting our borders, immigration reform, economic patriotism, fair trade, equal justice under law, restoring our lost sovereignty, putting America first—they are right out of the speeches we have been giving for eighteen months." The Republican party, he said, was turning into a "Buchanan party."

Perot Again

Meanwhile, the Reform Party was painstakingly laying the groundwork for its as-yet-unannounced presidential and vice presidential candidates to appear on the ballot in all fifty states in November. In July, Richard D. Lamm, a former governor of Colorado, announced that he would seek the party's presidential nomination. In short order, Ross Perot announced that he would, too.

After a complicated selection process that Lamm supporters and many observers thought unfairly favored Ross Perot, Perot accepted his party's presidential nomination on August 18.

Perot was harshly critical of both President Clinton and Republican candidate Bob Dole. (Quoting George Bush on "voodoo economics," Perot quipped that Dole's economic plan would put the country in "deep voodoo.") But his harshest criticism was reserved for the

Richard Lamm, in front of a Reform Party banner, was only briefly a candidate for the party's presidential nomination in 1996.

two-party system, which he contended had paralyzed and corrupted government. In his Reform Party nomination acceptance speech, Perot vowed to "kill that little snake this time."

Ross Perot was unlikely to win the election in November. In 1992, when he was a fresh face on the national political scene and much better liked as a public figure, he had won only 19 percent of the vote for president. However, as in 1992, if the race turned out to be a close one in November, he might pull enough votes away from one candidate or the other to affect the outcome. Both Dole and Clinton would have to take Perot and the Reform Party into account as they developed their campaign strategies.

In September, the Commission on Presidential Debates recommended that Perot not be allowed to participate in that fall's debates between the presidential candidates. The commission, made up of Republicans and Democrats, said that Perot didn't have a "realistic chance to win the election." Perot sued to join the debates, but lost. He aired a fresh round of television infomercials, but far fewer viewers tuned in to watch them than in 1992.

Election Day 1996

On November 5, President Clinton won reelection with 49.2 percent of the vote. Republican candidate Bob Dole trailed with 40.7 percent of the vote; Ross Perot received only 8.4 percent.

Perot and the Reform Party apparently didn't alter the outcome of the 1996 election. Pat Buchanan, by weakening Bob Dole and dividing the Republican party during the primary season, may have had a stronger effect.

However, Perot and the Reform Party were poised to become players in the 2000 election campaign. Because the Reform Party candidate for president won more than 5 percent of the vote in 1996, its candidate in 2000, whoever that turned out to be, would automatically be eligible to receive millions of dollars in federal campaign funds. In the future, Perot's coauthor and vice presidential running mate Pat Choate said on Election Day 1996, America's "policies and our governments will be dictated by a three-party system."

Chapter 5

Toward Election Day 2000

Undaunted by Ross Perot's defeat in the 1996 presidential election, in 1997 the Reform Party installed a set of party leaders loyal to Perot, including Russell J. Verney (Perot's 1996 campaign manager) as party chairman. A growing number of party activists grumbled that it was time for the Reform Party to move beyond being a vehicle for Ross Perot and to become a genuinely independent grassroots alternative to the Democratic and Republican parties. Perot and his supporters nonetheless remained firmly in control of the party's leadership.

Jesse Ventura

Ever since Ross Perot's 1992 presidential bid, candidates affiliated with Perot, United We Stand America, and the

Opposite:
During a press conference, Minnesota governor Jesse Ventura is adorned with his former trademarks—a feather boa and sunglasses—by wrestler Chyna.

Reform Party had been running for a few congressional seats as well as state and local offices around the country. The first of them to win a major office was Jesse Ventura, a former professional wrestler and radio personality who was elected governor of Minnesota on a Reform Party ticket in 1998. In an unusual eight-way race, Ventura won with only 37 percent of the vote.

Voters apparently found Ventura attractive for several reasons. He credibly claimed to be too inexperienced in politics to have been corrupted by it. He favored conservative government in economic matters and a hands-off, tolerant stance allowing individual choice on social issues such as abortion and gay rights. And, in a time of prosperity with no great crises requiring serious leadership, Ventura offered great entertainment value.

Ventura's surprising win in 1998, his colorful personality, and his unusual personal history attracted national attention and made him, after Perot, the Reform Party's second most prominent figure. Soon he and Perot were locked in a struggle for control of the party. (Ventura drew much of his support from the folks who thought it was time for the party to move beyond Ross Perot. Many of them had favored Richard Lamm instead of Perot for the Reform Party nomination in 1996.) In July 1999, delegates at a Reform Party national convention elected a new, Ventura-backed party chairman (Jack Gargan) over Perot's favored choice, the incumbent Russell J. Verney.

But Verney didn't leave office right away. He and other Perot supporters retained control of the party's national leadership through the end of 1999. In September, Verney called on Jesse Ventura to leave the Reform Party after Ventura, in an interview with *Playboy* magazine, said that "organized religion is a sham and a crutch for weak-minded people who need strength in numbers."

A Brief Look at Jesse Ventura

The boy who would become Jesse Ventura was born James George Janos on July 15, 1951, in Minneapolis, Minnesota. His father was a steamfitter working for the city of Minneapolis, his mother a nurse anesthetist. He attended public schools in Minneapolis. Right after high school, he joined the U.S. Navy, was trained as a SEAL (an elite team of Navy commandos), and served in the Navy for six years. In 1973, he returned home to Minnesota and attended a local community college for one year.

By 1975, he was wrestling professionally under the stage name Jesse "The Body" Ventura. In the colorful world of professional wrestling, the 6'4" Ventura wore rhinestone-spangled costumes and feather boas onstage. Beginning in 1984, Ventura acted in small parts in several movies, most notably Arnold Schwarzenegger's *Predator* in 1987. More steadily, he was a radio announcer and talk show host for much of the 1980s and 1990s.

In 1990, Ventura was elected mayor of Brooklyn Park, Minnesota, in which office he served for four years. In an upset victory in 1998, he was elected governor of Minnesota. That term of office runs through 2002.

Jesse Ventura's wife of more than two decades, Terry, has run her own horseback riding school. They have two children, Tyrel and Jade.

After the inauguration ceremony the new governor of Minnesota poses with, from left, daughter Jade, wife Terry, and son Tyrel.

"Your comments in . . . *Playboy*," Verney said, "about religion, sexual assault, overweight people, drugs, prostitution, women's undergarments and many other subjects do not represent the values, principles or ethics upon which this party was built.... You have brought shame to yourself and disgrace to the members of the Reform Party."

Through a smiling spokesman, Ventura conveyed a one-word response: "Pffff!"

Buchanan Again

In March 1999, Pat Buchanan announced that he would seek the Republican presidential nomination once again. His campaign speeches that spring and summer touched on themes familiar from his 1992 and 1996 presidential bids, calling for a protectionist "America first" trade policy, a legal ban on abortion, an end to affirmative action and bilingual education, and a freeze on immigration.

Buchanan's campaign was soon eclipsed by Texas Governor George W. Bush, son of former president George Bush. Governor Bush quickly raised tens of millions of dollars for his campaign and became the Republicans' presumptive nominee by midsummer—half a year before the first primary elections would be held in February 2000. (The race for the Democratic nomination, meanwhile, ended with strong support for Vice President Al Gore over former basketball player and senator Bill Bradley.) The Buchanan campaign was further hampered by controversy over a new book by Buchanan that questioned whether the United States should have gone to war against Nazi Germany. (The book, *The Great Betrayal: How American Sovereignty and Social Justice Are Being Sacrificed to the Gods of the Global Economy*, focused mostly on present-day economic and foreign policy.)

Who Will Be the Reform Party Candidate?

The Reform Party, meanwhile, began to consider who would be its candidate for president. Jesse Ventura ruled out running for president in 2000—but not, perhaps, in 2004. He and his supporters began looking for a well-known public figure who agreed with Ventura's political positions (conservative on economics, live-and-let-live on social issues) and who had the potential to win at least 5 percent of the vote for president—enough to qualify the Reform Party for a fresh award of federal campaign funds in 2004. Lowell Weicker, a former governor of Connecticut, and retired General Colin Powell were both approached, and both declined. Billionaire real estate baron Donald Trump met with Ventura in early fall 1999 and said he was considering whether to run.

Somewhere along the line, Pat Buchanan began to consider seeking the Reform nomination himself. While he had virtually no chance of winning the Republican nomination, his nationwide organization gave him a huge advantage in the Reform nomination process. And, perhaps decisively, Ross Perot apparently favored Buchanan for the nomination. (Perot's former running mate Pat Choate enthusiastically pursued Buchanan and paved the way for him to jump parties.) With Perot's silent nod and Buchanan's own political resources, Buchanan would be front-runner for the Reform Party nomination. If he won it, he would control the Reform Party's $12.6 million in 2000 federal campaign funds—enough to keep his message in the public eye all the way to November.

Buchanan Jumps—And So Does Trump

On October 25, 1999, Pat Buchanan announced that he was leaving the Republican Party and seeking the Reform Party's nomination for president in 2000. Speaking at a suburban hotel near his home outside Washington, D.C., Buchanan was cheered by a crowd of his own supporters as well as Reform Party state chairmen and local activists from around the country.

As a Reform Party candidate, Buchanan began to emphasize ideas and issues that especially appeal to Reform Party voters. He said that both he and the Reform Party stand for:

- "economic patriotism,"
- "a foreign policy that keeps America out of wars that are none of our business,"
- "restoring the full sovereignty and independence of the United States," and
- "political reform, campaign finance reform, opening up the system to other people and other parties."

But there were other issues that Pat Buchanan cared about deeply: "social and cultural conservatism" (the "cultural war" he'd spoken about since 1992) and abortion, which Buchanan believed should be outlawed. Both Buchanan and Perot-backed Reform Party leaders pointed out that the Reform Party did not take stands on these issues but instead sought to unite people who agreed on the need for political and economic reform even if they disagreed about other things. However, Jesse Ventura and his allies in the party noted that Reform Party voters mostly had a do-your-own-thing attitude toward social issues, preferring that government not get involved in such personal matters as abortion and homosexuality. Even if the *party* didn't officially disagree with Buchanan on these issues, its *voters* did.

On the very day that Buchanan jumped to the Reform Party, so did Donald Trump, by officially registering as a member of the Reform Party. (He, too, was formerly a Republican.) Trump, who had recently called

Buchanan a "Hitler lover" with "prehistoric" views on social issues, said that his own views were a better fit for the Reform Party than Buchanan's. He told reporters that he'd decide by early 2000 whether to seek the Reform Party nomination for president. "I would only do this if I felt I could win the election," he said.

It was hard to believe that Donald Trump could really be elected president of the United States in November

Billionaire developer Donald Trump joined the Reform Party in October 1999 and said he was considering seeking the party's presidential nomination.

2000. However, Trump did have a new book of memoirs due out in January 2000—just about when he said he'd decide whether to go for it. It was widely believed that Trump's flirtation with the Reform Party nomination was a publicity stunt, floated by Trump (a world-class promoter) to keep himself in the news and spur sales of his book.

Toward 2000—and Beyond

In February 2000, Trump announced that he had decided not to run for president that year—and Jesse Ventura announced that he was quitting the Reform Party's national organization. "The national party is going in directions that are not conducive to what we believe here in Minnesota and what we want the party to be," Ventura said. The very next day, Ventura's allies in the Reform Party's national leadership were forced out by supporters of Ross Perot and Pat Buchanan. Buchanan remained the front-runner for the party's presidential nomination.

But what about Ross Perot? He was getting close to seventy years old, and his family reportedly did not want him to run for president again. Throughout 1999, Perot had kept himself officially neutral and uninvolved in the race for the Reform Party nomination while people closely connected to him had strongly encouraged Buchanan to go for it. Heading into 2000, it looked unlikely that Perot would jump into the race himself. But Perot was notoriously unpredictable.

To win the Reform Party nomination for president according to the rules in early 2000, a candidate first had to try to get himself on the general-election ballot in the twenty-nine states (plus Washington, D.C.) where the Reform Party didn't already have ballot access secured. (In February 2000, Buchanan was the only candidate doing this. Given how difficult it is to get on many state's ballots, it was already all but too late for anyone else to attempt it.) In July 2000, the Reform Party's national leadership would determine which candidate(s) had made sufficient progress in securing ballot access, unless the party changes its rules in early 2000. A list of those candidate(s) would then be sent out for a vote. Based on the results of that vote, the Reform Party candidate for president would be proclaimed at a national convention in August.

Pat Buchanan looked overwhelmingly likely to win that nomination in August. In September and October, he would then have $12.6 million to spend in federal campaign funds earmarked for the Reform Party—plus free coverage on news programs and talk shows. If he did well enough in opinion polls (15 percent should do it), he might be included in the fall debates of presidential candidates. With Buchanan constantly in the public eye, getting his message out, the Democratic and Republican presidential candidates might be forced to address some of his (and the Reform Party's) favorite issues, such as reform of the American political system and what should be the rules for international trade.

Virtually no one expected Buchanan—or any Reform Party candidate—to win the presidency in November 2000. But it was a good bet that he'd win at least 5 percent of that vote. (Polls in late 1999 projected that Buchanan would get close to twice that in a three-way race.) In a close election, that might be enough to tip the balance and determine who will be the winner. Since Buchanan's original base of supporters was Republican, a sizable vote for Buchanan could hurt the Republican candidate. But if Buchanan continued to emphasize issues of economic justice, he might pull working-class voters away from the Democratic party, too.

Assuming the Reform Party did win at least 5 percent of the vote for president in 2000, under current federal campaign finance law the party would receive millions of dollars in funding for the 2004 presidential race. If it managed to win at least 25 percent of the vote in 2000, it would receive as much funding as the Democratic and Republican parties in 2004—an even three-way split.

Will the Reform Party become America's next major political party? Will it become a permanent minor party, small in numbers but potentially big in influence? Or will it fall apart amid arguments in its ranks? What happens in the year 2000 would shape the Reform Party's future—and perhaps even determine whether it would have any future at all.

Chronology

Feb.-Mar. 1992 Despite Pat Buchanan's surprisingly strong showing in the New Hampshire primary in early February, incumbent President George Bush effectively wraps up the Republican presidential nomination by early March.

Mar. 18, 1992 Ross Perot affirms that he'll run for president as an independent candidate if his supporters get him on the ballot in all fifty states.

July 16, 1992 Perot drops out of the presidential race.

Aug. 17, 1992 Buchanan addresses Republican National Convention, warning of a "cultural war" under way in America.

Oct. 1, 1992 Perot reenters the presidential race.

Nov. 2, 1992 Democrat Bill Clinton is elected president. Ross Perot receives 19 percent of the vote.

1993 Both Ross Perot and Pat Buchanan attack the proposed North Atlantic Free Trade Agreement (NAFTA), approved by Congress late this year.

Aug. 1995 Ross Perot's organization United We Stand America (soon to be the Reform Party) hosts a meeting of presidential hopefuls.

Feb.-Mar. 1996 Pat Buchanan, running for the Republican presidential nomination again, wins the New Hampshire Republican primary, but Bob Dole soon wins enough other contests to lock up the nomination.

July 1996 Former governor of Colorado Richard D. Lamm announces that he'll seek the Reform Party nomination for president. Ross Perot announces that he's seeking the nomination again himself.

Aug. 18, 1996 Perot accepts the Reform Party's presidential nomination.

Nov. 5, 1996 President Clinton wins reelection; Ross Perot gets 8.4 percent of the vote.

Nov. 1998 Jesse Ventura is elected governor of Minnesota, the first Reform Party candidate to win a major office.

July 1999	Delegates at a Reform Party national convention elect a party chairman backed by Jesse Ventura over Ross Perot's favored choice.		Republican Party and seeking the Reform Party 2000 presidential nomination.
Summer 1999	Pat Buchanan, whose bid for the 2000 Republican presidential nomination has stalled, begins to consider seeking the Reform Party nomination instead.	Feb. 2000	Jesse Ventura quits the Reform Party's national organization. Donald Trump announces that he has decided not to run for president in 2000.
Early Fall 1999	Encouraged by Jesse Ventura, real estate tycoon Donald Trump announces that he's considering seeking the Reform Party's 2000 presidential nomination.	July 2000	Reform Party officials determine which candidates get placed on a ballot for the party's presidential nomination.
Oct. 25, 1999	Pat Buchanan announces that he's leaving the	Aug. 2000	The Reform Party officially announces its presidential and vice presidential candidates at a party convention.
		Nov. 7, 2000	Election Day.

For Further Reading

Books

Buchanan, Patrick J. *Right From the Beginning*. Washington: Regnery Gateway, 1990.

Perot, Ross. *My Life and the Principles for Success*. Arlington, Texas: Summit Publishing Group, 1996.

Ventura, Jesse. *I Ain't Got Time to Bleed: Reworking the Body Politic From the Bottom Up*. New York: Villard Books, 1999.

Web sites

www.gopatgo2000.com — Pat Buchanan's official website.

www.pbs.org/newshour — Search here for PBS's extensive *NewsHour* 2000 election coverage.

www.reformparty.org — The Reform Party's official website.

Author's Note on Sources

Much of this book derives from research I did for Elizabeth Drew's "Letter from Washington" coverage of the 1992 presidential campaign for *The New Yorker* and for my own brief bios of Perot and Buchanan and coverage of the 1996 campaign and subsequent political developments for two CD-ROM programs, Broadcast News and Newslines (Primary Source Media, 1994–1998). For additional basic factual information, I relied mostly on the weekly Facts on File news digests (1991–1999) and on PBS's *NewsHour* and *The New York Times*, especially concerning the latter part of 1999. To flesh out the story, I also consulted Buchanan and Reform Party Web sites, assorted articles, and a dozen or so books by and about Buchanan, Perot, and the Reform Party.

The excerpts quoted in sidebars throughout the book come from these sources: In Chapter 1, *My Life and the Principles for Success*, by Ross Perot (Arlington, Texas: Summit Publishing Group, 1996); in Chapter 2, *Right From the Beginning*, by Patrick J. Buchanan (Washington: Regnery Gateway, 1990); in Chapter 3, Buchanan's speech as posted in early October 1999 on the www.gopatgo2000.com Web site, and *United We Stand: How We Can Take Back Our Country*, by Ross Perot (New York: Hyperion, 1992); in Chapter 4, letter from Ross Perot in United We Stand America's October 1995 "National Newsletter," and Buchanan's speech as posted in early October 1999 on the www.gopatgo2000.com Web site.

Index